BRITAIN SINCE 1930

JANE SHUTER

Heinemann

www.heinemann.co.uk
Visit our website to find out more information about Heinemann books.

To order:
☎ Phone 44 (0) 1865 888020
📄 Send a fax to 44 (0) 1865 314091
💻 Visit the Heinemann Bookshop at www.heinemann.co.uk to browse our catalogue and order online.

First published in Great Britain by Heinemann Library, Halley Court, Jordan Hill, Oxford OX2 8EJ, a division of Reed Educational and Professional Publishing Ltd. Heinemann is a registered trademark of Reed Educational & Professional Publishing Ltd.

OXFORD MELBOURNE AUCKLAND JOHANNESBURG BLANTYRE
GABORONE IBADAN PORTSMOUTH (NH) USA CHICAGO

Designed by Celia Floyd
Originated by Dot Gradations
Printed in Italy by LEGO

05 04 03 02 01
10 9 8 7 6 5 4 3 2 1
ISBN 0 431 10207 4 (hardback)

05 04 03 02 01
10 9 8 7 6 5 4 3 2 1
ISBN 0 431 10216 3 (paperback)

British Library Cataloguing in Publication Data

Shuter, Jane
    Britain since 1930. – (Exploring history)
    1. Great Britain – History – 20th century
    I. Title
    941'.084

Acknowledgements

The Publishers would like to thank the following for permission to reproduce photographs: Chris Honeywell: Pg.17; Corbis: Pg.22, Pg.24, Pg.26, Pg.29; Emma Robertson and Magnet Harlequin: pg.16; Greg Evans: Pg.27; Hulton: Pg.5, Pg.6, Pg.7, Pg.8, Pg.9, Pg.10, Pg.11, Pg.12, Pg.15, Pg.19; John Frost Newspapers: Pg.20; London Aerial Photo Library: Pg.23; PA News: Pg.18; Photofusion: Pg.25; REPP rights – unknown: Pg.13; Rex Features: Pg.21.

Cover photograph reproduced with permission of The Bridgeman Art Library.

Every effort has been made to contact copyright holders of any material reproduced in this book. Any omissions will be rectified in subsequent printings if notice is given to the Publisher.

Any words appearing in the text in bold, **like this**, are explained in the glossary.

Contents

What was it like for children in the Second
World War?

How has life in Britain changed since 1948?

What was it like for children in the Second World War?

What was the Second World War?

The Second World War lasted from 1939 to 1945. It involved countries from all over the world (although not every single country was involved). The Second World War, like most wars, was fought over land. Most of the fighting took place in Europe and Asia. There were also battles in North Africa and at sea in the Atlantic and Pacific Oceans.

Europe and North Africa

Germany had lost the First World War (1914–18). The **Treaty of Versailles** that ended the war took land away from Germany, and forced it to pay 'reparations' (compensation) to the victorious **Allies**. Most Germans (and some Allies) thought the treaty was too harsh.

The Nazi Party, led by Adolf Hitler, came to power in Germany in 1933. The Nazis wanted to re-gain land taken from Germany. In 1938 they took over Austria and Czechoslovakia. Their army was strong and fast moving. Hitler became set not just on getting back lost land but on taking over all of Europe. Britain and France declared war on Germany in September 1939. This part of the war was fought in Europe and North Africa. The various armies fought using guns and tanks. The air forces fought in the air and also bombed enemy cities. At sea the navies fought over and patrolled the shipping lanes and submarines sank enemy ships.

Asia

Meanwhile, in Asia, the Japanese had been trying to take over China since 1937. On 7 December 1941 the Japanese bombed the US fleet at Pearl Harbor. The next day Britain and the USA declared war on Japan and Hitler declared war on the USA.

The war in Europe ended on 8 May 1945, when Germany surrendered to the Allies. The war in Asia dragged on until 15 August 1945. The Japanese surrendered only after two atomic bombs had been dropped on the Japanese cities of Hiroshima and Nagasaki.

Adolf Hitler

Adolf Hitler (1889–1945) was born in Austria, the son of a poor customs official. In 1919 he joined the German Workers' Party. By 1921 he was in charge and renamed it the National Socialist German Workers' Party (Nazis for short). By 1932 the Nazi party was the biggest party in the German Parliament. Hitler became Chancellor in Germany in 1933 and quickly passed laws that meant that the Nazis were the only party in Germany and that Hitler could be the only leader. Hitler and the Nazis then swept Germany to war. The Nazis spread quickly across Europe, but in 1944 the Allies began to push the German army into retreat. On 29 April 1945 the Russians captured Berlin. Hitler killed himself the next day.

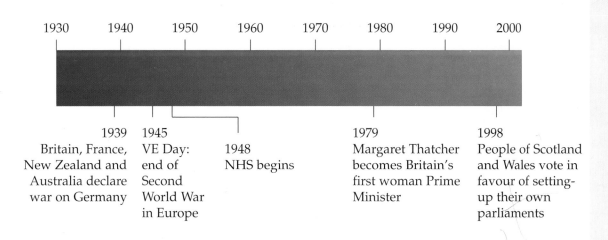

| 1930 | 1940 | 1950 | 1960 | 1970 | 1980 | 1990 | 2000 |

1939
Britain, France, New Zealand and Australia declare war on Germany

1945
VE Day: end of Second World War in Europe

1948
NHS begins

1979
Margaret Thatcher becomes Britain's first woman Prime Minister

1998
People of Scotland and Wales vote in favour of setting-up their own parliaments

Exploring further

The Heinemann Explore CD-ROM will give you extra information about Britain since 1930. From the Contents screen you can click on the blue words to find out about the Second World War and life in Britain since the war.

5

What was the Blitz?

The **Blitz** is the name given to the heavy bombing of Britain by the German Luftwaffe (air force) from September 1940 to May 1941. It was called the 'Blitz' as a short version of the German word 'blitzkrieg' a word applied to the fast and very heavy attacks the Germans made as they invaded other countries as well as to their bombing raids.

The first months of the war are often called 'the Phoney War' because people were waiting for attacks that did not come. German planes began to bomb ships to and from Britain, then military sites and factories. Then, on 6 September 1940, the German bombers launched their first large-scale attack on a British city – London. From then on they launched devastating attacks on Britain's cities, night after night, not targeting factories or military bases, but simply bombing whole cities and their people.

Civilian deaths

During the Blitz over 80,000 **civilians** were killed, more than half of the total of civilians killed in Britain during the whole war. The thing that made the Blitz (and the British bombings of German cities which followed) so shocking was that, for the first time, it was civilians, not factories or military buildings, that were the targets.

The **Luftwaffe** bombed large cities and ports, like London, Hull and Liverpool. The most destructive raid was on the city of Coventry on the night of 14 November 1940. Over 60,000 of the city's 75,000 buildings were destroyed or severely damaged, including the cathedral.

Winston Churchill

Winston Churchill (1874–1965), (seen here centre with a cigar) was born at Blenheim Palace in 1874. He became an MP in 1900. During the First World War (1914–18), he did various government jobs running the armed forces. From 1929 onwards, Churchill warned that the rise of dictators such as Hitler meant another war. He replaced Neville Chamberlain as Prime Minister in 1940. Many people saw Winston Churchill as the voice of Britain during the war because of the speeches he made to keep people going, particularly during the Blitz. Churchill and the Conservative Party lost the 1945 general election but were re-elected in 1951. By this stage, however, he was old and ill, and in 1955 he resigned as Prime Minister.

The Blitz was intended to make the British people sick of war and ready to give in to a German invasion. It did have a huge impact on people's lives. Many Londoners took to sheltering in Underground stations; some of them spent almost all their time there. It also made the British more determined to resist.

Exploring further – The Blitz

Follow this path to discover more about the Blitz:

World War II > Exploring > Invasion and Warfare > The Blitz

Click on the pictures to the left of the screen to make them bigger.

Why were children evacuated?

The government was sure that Germany would attack Britain as soon as war was declared. It made plans to **evacuate** mothers and pre-school children, schoolchildren and their teachers and disabled people from industrial cities, which they thought the Germans would attack first. They used the radio and poster campaigns to explain why evacuation was necessary. Some parents sent their children to relatives or friends in safe areas. Some decided to keep their families together, no matter what.

Evacuation problems

On 1 September 1939, two days before war broke out, the first government evacuation began. Despite the fact that the government had planned the evacuation a long time ahead, not everything went smoothly. Things could, and did, go wrong. Many **billeting** officers just told **host families** to come down to the station or village hall and 'help themselves'. Some trains arrived to find they were not expected.

The British government evacuated children for two reasons. Firstly, and most importantly, it kept them safe and reduced the likely numbers killed in bombing attacks. Secondly, it freed their mothers to go out and do war work. This reason became more important as the war went on and more and more men were **conscripted** into the armed forces.

In September 1939, children arrived at school with one case and a packed lunch and were labelled and led to the railway station. During the first three days of September almost 1,500,000 people were evacuated.

When months passed without a German attack, evacuees began to trickle back home. The trickle became a flood as Christmas came. By January 1940 about half of all the evacuees had gone home again.

German attack

In May, German bombers began to attack Britain. At first, they attacked factories and docks. At the same time, their troops moved through Belgium and France. By June 1940 Britain and her overseas colonies were the only **Allied** countries not occupied by the German Army and the Germans were in France, ready to invade Britain.

Now there was clearly real danger, a second evacuation to the countryside began. Factories and their workers were also moved into 'safe' areas. This evacuation had all the problems of the first and people began to go home again.

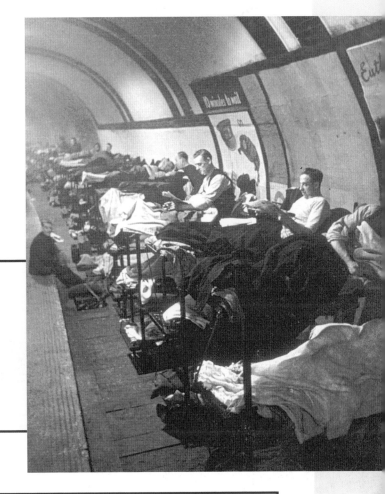

Shelter

During the bombings many people sheltered in underground stations. Some stations had bunks fitted although most people had to sleep crowded together on the platforms.

Exploring further – Work

The war had an effect on the way people worked. The CD-ROM tells you how the war affected adults and children.

World War II > Exploring > Everyday Life > Work

What was it like to be an evacuee?

Different **evacuees** had different experiences. Some evacuees from poor city homes went to friendly **host families** in the countryside and had a lovely time. There were real problems when they came home, because they wished they were back with their host family. Others had a miserable time and were even treated very cruelly. Most children, however, had experiences somewhere in between the two.

Some host families were shocked to find that their evacuees came from such poor homes that they had lice, fleas or infectious diseases. Some children from middle-class homes were shocked to find themselves in homes without a water supply or indoor toilets, where they were expected to work hard and sleep on a straw mattress on the floor. The evacuees and local children usually had a few problems at first, although in most cases things settled down.

These evacuees are being 'trained' to resist a German invasion! While games like this were common there was a level of seriousness about them too.

 Sheila Price was evacuated from London when she was twelve.

There was an orchard with fruit. We had a car to take us to school, a piano, a beautiful home, servants, typing lessons, mini-golf and a fine lawn. Most of all, the family was warm and understanding. I became a snob. Each weekend I went home on the bus. Our street looked dingy and poor. I hated it. Eventually, mother said I was to come home and look after the others. My lovely world crumbled.

L A M Brech, a teacher, remembers being evacuated just before war broke out.

All you could hear was the feet of the children and a kind of murmur because the children were too afraid to talk. When we got to the station we knew which platform to go to, the train was ready, but we hadn't the slightest idea where we were going. The mothers pressed against the iron gates calling 'Goodbye, darling'. I never see those gates at Waterloo without a lump coming to my throat.

There was a terrible shortage of space. A lot of evacuee kids had swollen the numbers. They were called 'vacs' or 'vakkies'. We were taught in the church hall across the road as well as the school. There were two classes in the hall at the same time, with just screens between. They'd be doing singing lessons on one side and trying to teach history on the other.

Adrian Walker remembers the effect of evacuees on his village school during the war.

Don't forget that walls have ears!

Men and women were **conscripted** into the armed forces. Their families were not allowed to know where their relatives were going. The government stressed that 'Careless Talk Costs Lives'; who knew if an enemy spy was listening?

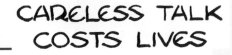

CARELESS TALK COSTS LIVES

Exploring further – Written sources

Letters and diaries tell us how children felt about evacuation. You can find some of these on the CD-ROM in the Written Sources section.

What did people eat during the war?

What people ate in the war varied, but most of the European countries involved in the war introduced some form of **rationing**. So people ate less, but often more healthily, than before the war. In some parts of Europe people began to starve.

Rationing

Before the war Britain bought about two-thirds of its food from other countries. But the war disrupted shipping and food supplies dried up. People began to miss the meat from Australia and sugar and fruit from the West Indies. The government introduced rationing, mainly because people wanted it – they thought it was fairer than 'first come, first served'.

Food rationing began in January 1940. At first it was just sugar (12 oz), butter (4 oz) and bacon (12 oz) that had a weekly ration. In March meat was rationed, and tea was added in July. The government provided babies and children with free milk and schools and factories provided hot meals in the middle of the day. The worst thing about rationing for many people, however, was that it went on after the war had ended. Bread was not rationed until after the war, sweet rationing went on until 1953 and rationing did not completely end until 1954.

Food shortage

Shortages and rationing did not mean that people starved. But they ate a limited range of foods and far less food than before the war. In 1944 people ate an eighth of the amount of food eaten in 1938.

An average week's ration for one adult during most of the war.

Meat	up to 1s 2d worth (s = shillings, d = pence)
	Sausages not rationed, but hard to get
Bacon and ham	4 oz
Butter	2 oz
Cheese	2 oz
Milk	3 pts
Margarine	4 oz
Cooking fat	2 oz
Sugar	8 oz
Jam/marmalade/pickles	8 oz a month in all
Eggs	1 a week
Dried egg	1 packet every 4 weeks
Sweets	4 oz a week

Lord Woolton was made Minister of Food in April 1940. He began to organize people to fight the war on 'the Kitchen Front'. People soon got used to posters like this urging them to grow their own food.

Land Army

The government made a big effort to get people to grow their own food. Farmers were encouraged to grow more grain and vegetables, just at a time when they had fewer workers. So the government set up the **Land Army**, which trained women to farm and then **billeted** them on farms to help with the work. Local councils also divided up patches of spare land into **allotments**.

Exploring further – Lord Woolton

Discover more about Lord Woolton's Ministry of Food on the CD-ROM:

World War II > Exploring > Key People and Events > Lord Woolton and the 'kitchen front'

In what other ways might the war have affected people?

Running the country

The war meant a lot of people were needed to organize wartime precautions and rescues, as well as ration books and all sorts of passes and permits that people began to need to travel around. Some of the jobs created to do this kind of organizing were:

- Civil Defence workers; fire wardens and fire fighters, first aid and ambulance workers and air-raid wardens.
- Local Defence Volunteers; called the Home Guard, they were people who could not join the army because of health or age. They were trained to fight a German invasion.
- Women's Voluntary Services; (the WVS) organized **canteens**, clothes and other help for people who were bombed out of their homes.

Work

Many men left their jobs and went to fight in the war. For the first year, some jobs were 'reserve occupations' – they were too important for men to leave to join the army.

Some women took over 'everyday' jobs – driving buses, delivering milk, working in offices. Some women joined the army, navy or air force. Others joined the **Land Army** and worked on farms or in factories. There were some jobs, like digging coal, that were still seen as too hard for women. This work was given to prisoners of war or **conscientious objectors**.

Family life

Some families found that the war disrupted their lives enormously. Perhaps they lost everything they had in bombing raids, or family members were killed either at home or in the fighting. Other families were less affected. The pattern of everyday life was disrupted by **air raids** and air-raid warnings. Many people lost their homes and many towns had at least some areas that were bombed into nothing but rubble.

Land Army

These Land Girls worked long hours on the farms, but were only paid about £20 per week.

Transport

The war affected travel in several ways. One big effect was that petrol **rationing** meant people travelled by car far less. After March 1942 ordinary people could only get petrol if they could prove their car was vital – doctors, for instance needed to be able to reach their patients.

Journeys were also complicated by government precautions to catch German spies. People needed travel passes to travel. Railway station names were painted out, so it was hard to tell where the train had stopped. Signposts on roads were taken down and put into store.

Exploring further – The effects of war

The war affected many other areas of life. Follow this path on the CD-ROM:

World War II > Key Questions > In what other ways might the war have affected people?

You'll find links to pages about the topic.

What were children's experiences of the war?

Children in different countries had different experiences of the war. These experiences depended on where they lived and what their nationality was. In areas taken over by the Germans it also depended on their religion.

Jews and Nazis

Jewish people and people of what the Nazis thought of as 'inferior' nationalities were treated very badly. Huge numbers were put into **concentration camps** in appalling living and working conditions, close to starvation. At worst they were killed in one of the several 'death camps' set up in Poland. Two children born next door to each other in Frankfurt, Germany would have had very different experiences of the war if one of those families was Jewish and the father of the other was a Nazi.

Hundreds of thousands of Jewish children did not survive the war, unless they and their parents became **refugees** early on and fled to another country. Even then, they needed to go far enough away – those who fled to Britain were safe; those who fled to Holland were not, because the Germans eventually occupied Holland.

Auschwitz

Millions of people were crammed into Auschwitz and other death camps. This is one of the huts where people slept at least 3 people to each 'sleeping shelf'.

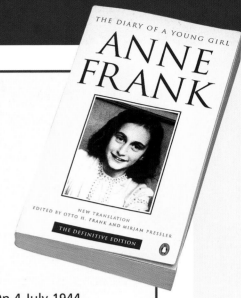

Anne Frank

Anne Frank (1929-1945) was born in Frankfurt, Germany but moved to Amsterdam, Holland, in 1933 when the Nazis came to power. In 1940 the Nazis took over Holland as well. Her father Otto Frank decided the family had to hide. He made a secret hiding place, the Annexe, in his offices. The Franks moved into the Annexe in July 1942. They hid there for two years. While they were in hiding Anne kept a diary, which is how we know about life in the Annexe. On 4 July 1944 the Nazis discovered the Annexe. They put the Franks and their friends in a Dutch prison camp. Then they were moved to Auschwitz camp in German-occupied Poland, where Edith died. Anne and Margot died in Belsen camp in Germany. Otto was the only survivor from the Annexe.

What was it like to be a child living in this area in the Second World War?

The answer to this question will depend where you live. You will need to do your own research for this.

To find this out you will need:
- Maps of your local area.
- Photos from the time.

Where you can find this information:
- Your local record office often produces packs to help with history projects.
- The nearest big public library often has local history collections and sometimes produces books or postcard packs of photos.
- Some families may have relatives who grew up in your area during the war. Some of these people might like to talk about their experiences.

Exploring further – Anne Frank

The Digging Deeper section of the CD-ROM allows you to find out more about the topics that interest you. There is lots of information about Anne Frank's life. Follow this path:

World War II > Digging Deeper > Anne Frank

What has been done since to prevent another world war?

Germany surrendered on 4 May 1945. People celebrated VE Day, but 'VE' only stood for 'Victory in Europe' - the Japanese were still fighting on. Many people had relatives who were fighting in the Pacific or imprisoned in Japanese **POW** camps. The **Allies** began to discuss using a new bomb they had developed: the atomic bomb. This was 2,000 times more powerful than any other single bomb.

President Truman of the USA decided to use the first atomic bomb on the city of Hiroshima on 6 August 1945. The Japanese still refused to surrender. So, three days later, another atomic bomb was dropped on the city of Nagasaki. The Japanese surrendered on 14 August 1945 but at the cost of millions of lives and mass destruction.

The Atomic Bomb

The scientists understood that atomic bombs could cause a huge amount of damage. However, few people fully understood the far-reaching effects the radiation released when the bomb exploded.

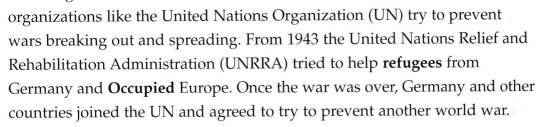

'Peacekeeping forces' like this one are made up of soldiers from different countries in the UN.

The United Nations

A third world war would be hugely destructive. Various governments and organizations like the United Nations Organization (UN) try to prevent wars breaking out and spreading. From 1943 the United Nations Relief and Rehabilitation Administration (UNRRA) tried to help **refugees** from Germany and **Occupied** Europe. Once the war was over, Germany and other countries joined the UN and agreed to try to prevent another world war.

The UN now has two different jobs. Firstly, it tries to prevent countries from fighting. Secondly it tries to help countries, especially developing countries, by giving economic and medical help. In 1960 the African country called the Congo became independent. There was fierce fighting between different groups who wanted to take power. The UN sent a 'peacekeeping force' of 20,000 soldiers, who stopped the fighting. However, UN intervention has not always helped to keep peace or stop civil war, for example in the countries of former Yugoslavia.

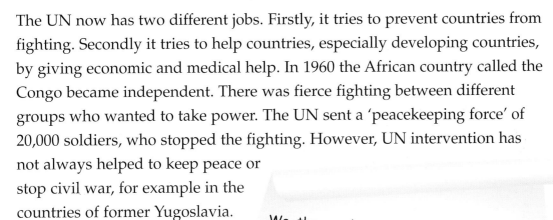

We, the peoples of the United Nations, are determined to save future generations from war and to reaffirm our faith in human rights. We believe in the dignity and worth of the human person, in the equal rights of men and women and nations large and small.

From the United Nations Organization's Charter, 1945.

Exploring further – The United Nations

Try searching for information about the United Nations. Click on Search, taking the World War II option and select the keyword UN.

How can we begin to find out about change since the Second World War?

A person from 1940s Britain would find it hard to believe that modern Britain was the same country. The landscape, buildings and countryside look different. People have changed too – there are many different races and they wear very different clothes. Who works, how and where they work, and how families live together would all surprise a person from the 1940s.

Some changes have been gradual; others have not – especially technological changes since the 1960s. Many of the things in the shops, especially electrical shops, would be hard to understand – not just computers but even things like irons! All the gadgets in a modern kitchen would overwhelm a housewife from the 1940s.

It is important when thinking about change since 1948 to ask yourself what you are going to investigate. The question needs to be broken up into chunks. First you need to break down the time span from the Second World War to the present day. Historians usually do this in decades – batches of ten years – the 1940s, the 1950s and so on. You also need to break up the question 'How has Britain changed since the Second World War?' You will find that many of the questions tie in with each other. This is because change is complicated and one change sets off several other changes.

Newspapers tell us about important changes in the past. They also tell us about what was important to the people at the time.

What types of evidence can we use to find out about life in Britain since the Second World War?

When you are trying to find out about change since the Second World War you can use the kinds of evidence that all historians use:

- Artefacts – things that people made at the time that have survived
- Written records – official documents, such as birth certificates, also newspapers and magazines
- Other written evidence – letters, diaries, posters
- Books – books written by historians and stories written at the time
- Maps – to show how the country has changed. A road map of Britain in 1948 looks very different from one produced now.
- Films
- Music
- Plays
- Photos and paintings
- You can use something that is not always available to historians – people who were there at the time. Although these people can only tell you about their own experience they can bring the recent past to life.

 Clothes, like these minidresses from the late 1960s, tell us about fashion. They also tell us about attitudes at the time.

Exploring further – Pictures as evidence

Use the CD-ROM to find out more about changes in Britain since 1948. To see a bank of pictures showing the way Britain has changed follow this path:

Social and Tech Change > Pictures > Change and Influences

Click on one of the pictures to make it bigger and find out what it shows.

What are the changes in work and home life since 1948? When did these changes happen?

How has work changed?

The Second World War changed the way people worked. It took a lot of people into the armed forces. Factories were set up to produce war goods – ammunition, tanks, planes and all sorts of other equipment.

 In the 1950s and 1960s more women were working than ever before in jobs such as nursing under the NHS.

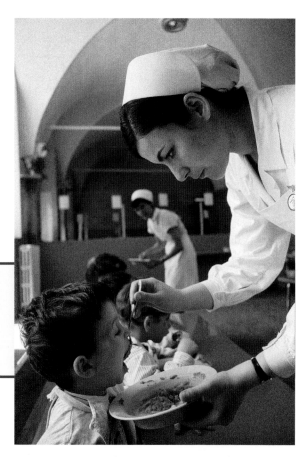

Over the 1950s and 1960s the jobs people did changed. Coal mining, cloth making and shipbuilding became less important. New industries grew, like those that produced new household goods. The car industry also expanded rapidly. More people worked in offices, including running the newly set up welfare state. Strong **trade unions** pushed for more pay and better conditions for workers. Workers began to strike when their employers refused to meet their demands.

Work since the 1970s

The 1970s were years when workers felt powerful. In 1972 the government had to introduce a three-day working week twice, because strikes by the miners led to severe coal shortages. The winter of 1979 became known as 'the winter of discontent' when almost everyone, including ambulance

This picture of Enfield, taken in 1997, shows a variety of homes, from two-storey houses with gardens to 1960s high-rise flats.

drivers and dustmen, went on strike. By the year 2000 there had been a drastic change in who was working, the work they did and where they worked. There were more **white-collar** workers than **blue-collar** workers. There were many more women workers, both married and single. More people worked flexible hours and computers allowed many people to work from home.

Changing families

In the 1940s people often lived in the same town all their lives, near their parents and families. As time has passed people have travelled further and further to find work. Families are scattered all over the country. While people still feel that they should care for elderly relatives, this care is more likely to be paying for them to go into a nursing home or have home help, rather than taking them into their own home.

Another change was brought about by changes in the law on divorce. In the 1940s there were very few divorces in Britain – it was difficult and was seen as something to be ashamed of. Changes in both law and attitudes meant that in 1965 there were about 37,800 divorces in Britain.

Exploring further – Motor cars

Affordable cars had a great effect on people's lives. Discover the man behind one of Britain's most popular cars:

Social and Tech Change > Biographies > Alec Issigonis

What are the changes in technology and popular culture since 1948? When did these changes happen?

Since the 1930s advances in technology have changed the way we live. The speed of change has been getting faster and faster ever since Harold Wilson, who became Prime Minister in 1964, announced that Britain would become brighter and more efficient thanks to 'the white heat of a technological revolution.'

By the 1960s Britain was 'swinging'. Britain was where the miniskirt and the Mini car began. Britain also produced pop music with world-wide appeal – like the Beatles.

A bright new future?

Computers have changed the way that people work and play. In the 1940s, although computers existed, few could imagine a time when they would be small and affordable enough for people to use in their own homes. Microprocessors were invented in 1971 to power computers. They were soon in use in all kinds of machines, including microwave ovens and self-defrost fridges.

Technological advances have had bad effects too. They have led to pollution and environmental problems. Nuclear fuel was seen as cleaner than fuels such as coal and oil and it would not run out. The first nuclear power stations were built in the 1950s. But nuclear power produces radioactive waste, which can be very dangerous. The number of nuclear power stations being built has declined in recent years.

How has popular culture developed?

Before the Second World War there was no real 'popular culture' – ideas, entertainment or activities that people from all social classes enjoyed. Even a day out that many different people went to, such as horse racing, split people into different groups. They might be watching the same races, but few of them were mixing with people from another class.

The war began a process of breaking down class barriers. Several things led to the creation of a popular culture – the most important of which were the 'throwaway culture', which brought fashion into most people's reach and the technological changes that brought TV and music into everyone's home.

The 'box' in the corner

During the war radio began to create a popular culture. Everyone could listen to the same programmes. After the war record players and records became cheaper. The music industry boomed as record players turned into hi-fi units and then, in the 1980s, CD players. The invention that encouraged popular culture the most was the TV. Many families bought their first TV to watch Queen Elizabeth II's coronation in 1953.

Mobile phones are the latest 'popular' technological advance. They allow people to stay in touch much more easily.

Exploring further – Television

Click on Search, taking the Social and Tech Change option. Select the keyword Television. You will see a list of pages that mention television and its effect on Britain.

What are the changes in Britain's population since 1948? When did these changes happen?

Britain's population has changed a lot since the 1940s. It has changed in several ways – ethnic mix, size and age balance.

 West Indian immigrants arriving in Britain in 1956. Early immigrants were welcomed in Britain because of the shortage of workers.

Getting bigger

In 1948 the population of Britain was about 47 million. In 1996 it was about 58 million. However, population growth is slowing down. Population figures are affected by more than the number of babies born. People **emigrating** from and **immigrating** to Britain affect these figures, as do the number of people living longer.

Getting more varied

There was a much wider ethnic mix (mix of people from different cultures) of people in Britain in 2000 than ever before. In the 1940s there were growing groups of non-white, non-Christian people in Britain. They tended to live in their own groups, mostly in the cities. There were probably not even a million of them by 1948.

After the war there was a shortage of workers, so immigrants were welcomed. As more immigrants arrived, more white people began to object. There had always been racial prejudice; now there were outbreaks of racial violence. The violence eventually slowed. While violence and prejudice still exist, the more varied society becomes the less it happens.

Donald Hinds

Donald Hinds (1937–) was born and brought up in Jamaica, in the West Indies. He emigrated to Britain in August 1955 and began working in London as a bus conductor. Donald went to college in his spare time. He wrote articles for newspapers and magazines and also worked for the BBC. In 1965 he wrote a book called *Journey to Illusion*, about the problems facing West Indians in Britain. Hinds joined the Open University and studied for a degree. He then became a teacher in a comprehensive school in South London. He married Dawn, a social worker, and they had three daughters.

Getting older

The 1931 **census** showed that the number of children born was dropping, while older people were living longer – the age balance of the population was changing. After the devastation of the war, the birth rate began to climb again which led to a youth culture in the 1960s and 1970s. By the 1980s and 90s the birth rate was falling again. Thanks to the National Health Service and advances in medicine, elderly people were living longer. The trend is expected to continue.

In 1998 19.1% of the population was under fourteen years old. In 2007 this is expected to have fallen to 17.6%.

By 1990, after decades of immigration, almost 10% of the British population was non-white or of mixed race.

Exploring further – Immigration

Read about the experiences of another person who came to Britain from the Caribbean. Follow this path:

Social and Tech Change > Biographies > Claudia Jones

What links and connections can we make between the changes in British life since 1948?

A good way to show how different changes link up is to make a big wall chart which lists the questions you have asked and gives very short (one or two words if possible) summaries of the answer. Then join the questions that have connections with different coloured marker pen lines or coloured string or ribbon. [*For example:* one of the answers to 'How did everyday life change?' could be 'People began to go abroad for holidays' – 'travel further' for short. This could link to one of the answers to 'What technological changes have there been?' – 'jet airplanes'.]

What have been the most important changes since 1948? How are those changes linked? It is important to remember when thinking about these questions is that there is not one right answer or set of answers. You are being asked to choose what you think. Some things may seem more obvious than other things, but the most important thing is to give a good reason for your choice.

 Ray Lomas, from Maidstone, feels that holidays abroad have changed a lot since he was a boy.

I remember when package holidays to Spain first came out. The family went on a package for two weeks. My dad said never again. They came back bright red and peeling, with upset tummies from the foreign food. Because then, abroad was different, really foreign and not many of the locals spoke English. We persuaded them to go with us to Torremolinos a few years ago. They were stunned by the difference. The people all spoke English, you could get fish and chips and Dad's favourite beer, Mum could even play Bingo. They're going back next year. We aren't. We like to look for places that are still different from England - they're getting harder and harder to find.

Children enjoying the Notting Hill Carnival in London in 1990.

Before you decide what your answer is you should ask yourself what makes a change important? Is it:

- something that affects a lot of people a bit
- something that affects a few people a lot
- something that affects all of Britain
- something that only affects part of Britain
- something beneficial
- something harmful
- something which will affect Britain for a long time?

Written by Michio Kaku in *Visions*, published in 1998.

In many ways the impact of the Internet is like the invention of moveable type in the 1450s, which meant large numbers of books could be printed for the first time. Before this there were only about 30,000 books in all of Europe. Only a few people owned books or could read. Books were a luxury and a tool that were jealously guarded. The Internet takes another step towards spreading information widely and quickly.

Exploring further – The computer

Read more about the development of computers on the CD-ROM:

Social and Tech Change > Exploring > Discoveries, Inventions and Ideas > The Computer

Timeline

1931	First Highway Code
1936	BBC demonstrates television at the Radio Exhibition in London
1937	Frozen food on sale in shops for the first time: peas, strawberries and asparagus, for example
1938	The German Army takes over Austria and the German-speaking parts of Czechoslovakia that once belonged to Germany
1939	The German Army takes over the rest of Czechoslovakia; Britain promises to defend Poland if Germany attacks
1 September 1939	The German Army marches into Poland; Britain begins first evacuation and blackout
3 September 1939	Britain, France, New Zealand and Australia declare war on Germany
23 September 1939	Petrol rationing begins in Britain
8 January 1940	Food rationing in Britain
2 June 1941	Clothing rationing in Britain
1 December 1942	William Beveridge publishes his Report on Social Security outlining a welfare state system for Britain
8 May 1945	VE Day: end of World War II in Europe
14 August 1945	Japan surrenders after atomic bombs are dropped on Hiroshima and Nagasaki
1948	NHS (National Health Service) begins
1951	Festival of Britain opens in London
1952	New 'pop music' paper, New Musical Express, publishes the first pop music chart of best selling records
1954	All rationing ends
1958	Race riots, Notting Hill, London
1962	The Beatles' first hit record, Love Me Do, enters the charts
1964	BBC2 begins broadcasting
1966	Barclays Bank introduce Barclaycard – the first ever credit card
1971	Britain changes to decimal currency
1979	Margaret Thatcher becomes Britain's first woman Prime Minister
1998	People of Scotland and Wales vote in favour of setting-up their own parliaments

Glossary

air raids attack by enemy aircraft; particularly bombing

Allies all the countries that fought against Germany during the Second World War

allotments rented plots of council land used to grow vegetables

billeted to be sent somewhere to live and work

billeting officer someone in charge of finding soldiers, refugees or evacuees places to stay

Blitz short for the German word 'blitzkrieg' meaning 'lightning war', used to describe the constant bombing raids of Britain by Germany from September 1940 to May 1941

blue-collar (workers) term for people who work with their hands, in factories or other trades. It refers to wearing blue overalls, not white shirts to work.

canteen a place that serves food for the homeless, or people working in a school, office or factory

census a count of all the people in the country on a particular day

civilians people who are not members of any of the armed forces

concentration camp a prison where political prisoners could be held; in practice ill-treatment and torture was common

conscientious objectors people who will not fight because it is against their beliefs

conscripted/conscription being made to join the armed forces

emigrating leaving one country to live permanently in another

evacuate/evacuation moving people out of a place that has become, or will become, dangerous

evacuees people who are evacuated

host families a family that takes in evacuees or other people

immigrating coming to live in one country from another country, usually the one you were born in

Land Army most people in the Land Army were women who were trained and moved around the country to work on farms that needed extra workers

Luftwaffe the German airforce

Occupied countries in Europe under German control during the Second World War, for example France and Holland

POW prisoners of war; soldiers who had been captured

rationing fixing the amount of food, petrol or other goods that people can buy

refugees people who had fled a place because of religious or political persecution by the people there

trade union organization to protect and improve the rights of workers

Treaty of Versailles official agreement between different countries

white-collar (workers) term used for people who work in offices. It refers to them wearing white shirts to work rather than blue overalls.

Index